CW00548846

ALL THE BUILDINGS*
IN
PARIS

*THAT I'VE DRAWN SO FAR
BY JAMES GULLIVER HANCOCK

UNIVERSE

INTRODUCTION

JAMES GULLIVER HANCOCK

I only have to say the word "Paris" and it conjures up very strong emotions and aesthetic associations in people across the globe. The implications of this name are so universal that I almost need not even put pencil to paper - it's all there in our heads right after we hear "Paris", everything from classic food to fine art masters, fashion, and even pure romance itself. It is amazing that a city can lay claim to so much strong symbolism in popular culture.

It is hard then to step away from all the clichés Paris holds in its grasp. When I visited Paris, I had a similar experience to first being in New York. What can I do to really experience this place? I didn't want to just wander around taking photos and eating chocolate croissants wishing I'd grown up hanging out in cafés with Jean-Paul Sartre or Picasso. It's frustrating visiting a place that is obviously so important. Paris is so well-known that people often have a preconceived map of the city in their head, before they visit in person. The thing, then, is to re-map a place for yourself. To separate myth from reality. I do this with drawing.

I use drawing in an attempt to squeeze out as much from those single-moment observations as I can to understand place and its associations more personally. It feels sort of like giving the place a big long hug when I get it right. I turn to buildings because they are the fabric that make up the place that holds all these experiences and associations together. They are silent observers through the ages, gathering the dust of poetry, violence, and romance over each decade.

It is amazing that inanimate objects can hold such romantic symbols in their static standing walls. We embue them with so much history and significance that they become alive.

I first arrived in Paris at the end of a huge overland journey from Sydney, Australia, to Paris, France. I stepped into a familiar storybook, it seemed. The language, the food, the street names, the Seine, the buildings, the paintings on the wall of the Louvre were all familiar from an alternate universe of fiction I'd read about back home. The whole reason I do these projects on the buildings of cities is to properly understand the places so as to overcome exactly that sensation of being in a fantasy. Drawing each experience of place I have in a city helps me more effectively log an understanding of it. It makes me stop and look and really take it all in. If I'd just taken a

ALL THE ROOFTOPS IN PARIS

photo I wouldn't have seen the little details all the way at the top; the smiling gargoyle or the smell of that particular street might not have overwhelmed me as I drew. When you spend time in one place, you form very strong memories about it that you can savor for life, and can relive through these diary-like drawings.

After my first visit I returned to Paris to live for a while. I was invited to stay at la Cité Internationale des Arts just near the Marais. It was a magical time. My girlfriend (now wife) and I would wake up to the sound of opera singers in the studio next door. We would then head to the market, we loved getting whole trout to grill and fresh strawberries and blue cheese so funky it was like eating an opiate.

The key drawing I did when I was at the Cité was the one on this spread, "All the Rooftops in Paris". It was one of my first attempts to document the things I liked in a city. I was sitting on top of Sacré Coeur one day looking at all those rooftops and I was overwhelmed by the layers of built structures lapping over one another and arching in an almost organic growth of chimneys and tiles and little windows. So I started drawing, and I began looking up on every street and seeing such amazing eclectic structures on the top of buildings, I wanted to collect them all. Then my obsessive nature took over and all I could see was this fascinating patchwork quilt of structures, all joined together and chatting like old friends.

For me, Parisian architecture is inextricably linked to food experiences. It's the way the awnings arched over the displays of the best cheese I'd ever tasted, the little hole-in-the-wall crêpe place that blew my mind with my first lemon and sugar crêpe. Of course, there are the decorative pàtisserie counters you can never find again that had a life-changing pain au chocolate and baguettes that don't taste the same anywhere else. Specifically I remember the best chocolate cake I've ever tasted in the patisserie around the corner from where I stayed. It was a cinematic moment when I tasted it, almost religious, as if all my senses opened wide and I could see all the details around me. I'll never forget the building it was in and the pavement out front, the regular supermarket next door, the gruff lady that served me, and the pure drug-addict-like disappointment when they never seemed to have that cake again. Drawing is a way to capture those fleeting poetic moments. For me drawing allows a moment in time when a pure experience of the present comes out of your body and onto the page in the only way it can at that time. It will never be the same again. Drawing seems to log it the most effectively for me.

It's amazing how different senses can form really strong memories. Mostly the sticky memories happen by accident, when you unexpectedly bite into that cake, or a whiff of cheese floats by. Drawing typically forces a more consistent achievement of memorized moments. Drawing makes you stop, look, and physically interact with the things around and in front of you. By drawing, reality flows through your eyes, your brain, your muscles, your fingers, and onto the page. All parts of your body are engaged and influence the diary-like moment of drawing. The chair you sit in is in that drawing; those high heels on the cobble stones you can hear are as well. So I end up falling in love with a place through drawing—you see it, you grab it, and it's almost like you own a version of it from then on.

I encourage you to explore your place through drawing - the more you stop and look, the more you see and experience. Having a healthy dose of obsession is definitely important; repeatedly viewing the same things brings a different knowledge. It also spurs you on to embrace as much as you can. The anxiety of not seeing all of Paris was the impetus behind the attempt to draw all the buildings, a sort of promise to myself that at some stage I would experience everything this divine place has to offer. I find the almost infinite nature of the project's title reassuring, even if it is impossible or ridiculous.

I am always drawing, and hence I'm always looking. Paris, like a lot of places I've visited, will always be with me because I took time to stop and look and observe how it works. My obsession with representing what is around me is endlessly entertaining for me and I hope the results in this book are for you as well.

My obsession continues with this project at www.allthebuilldingsinparis.com

6 PARVIS
NOTRE-DAME

NOTRE-DAME
(OUR LADY)

ONE OF THE FINEST
EXAMPLES OF FRENCH
GOTHIC ARCHITECTURE.

ONE OF THE FIRST BUILDINGS
TO USE FLYING BUTTRESSES

BUILT BETWEEN
1160 - 1345

ÎLE DE LA CITÉ

IT WAS THE RESIDENCE
OF THE KING OF
FRANCE FROM THE
6TH-14TH CENTURIES.
DURING THE
REVOLUTION IT WAS
A COURTHOUSE AND
PRISON.

TRACES OF HUMAN
HABITATION HAVE BEEN
FOUND AND DATED
TO 5000 BC.

PALAIS
DE LA CITÉ

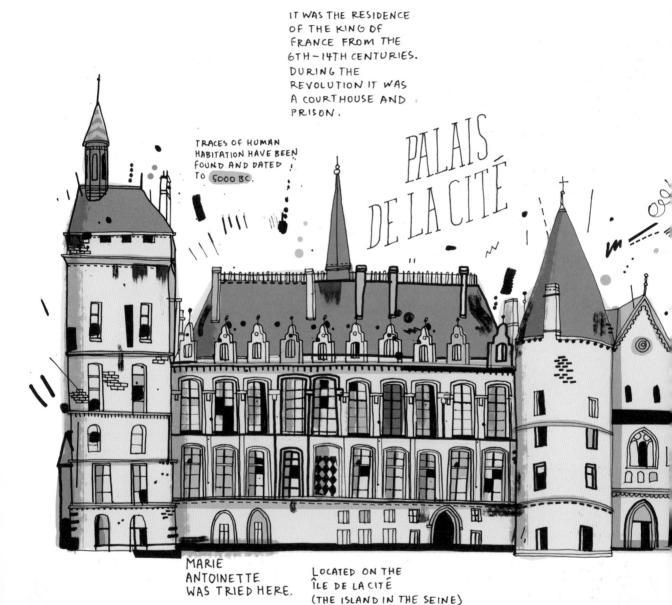

MARIE
ANTOINETTE
WAS TRIED HERE.

LOCATED ON THE
ÎLE DE LA CITÉ
(THE ISLAND IN THE SEINE)

WORLD'S LARGEST MUSEUM

8 RUE DES HALLES

"DESTRUCTION OF HARMFUL ANIMALS" OPEN SINCE 1872

DESTRUCTION des ANIMAUX NUISIBLES

DEAD RATS!

ST.-
EUSTACHE
2 IMPASSE
SAINT-EUSTACHE

NAMED AFTER A ROMAN GENERAL WHO WAS KILLED FOR CONVERTING TO CHRISTIANITY

A MASTERPIECE OF GOTHIC ARCHITECTURE

BUILT BETWEEN 1532 - 1632

GREEN PIPES
ARE PLUMBING

BLUE DUCTS
ARE FOR AIR
CONDITIONING

YELLOW IS FOR
ELECTRICITY

RED IS FOR
CIRCULATION

CENTRE GEORGES POMPIDOU

OPENED IN 1977

THE BUILDING IS CONSTRUCTED INSIDE
WITH ALL THE UTILITIES ON THE OUTSIDE.

DESIGNED BY:
RICHARD ROGERS
RENZO PIANO
GIANFRANCO FRANCHINI

BUILT FROM 1509-23

TOUR SAINT-JACQUES

52 METERS ·HIGH (**170** FEET) THIS TOWER IS ALL THAT REMAINS OF A FORMER **16**TH-CENTURY CHURCH THAT WAS DESTROYED DURING THE FRENCH REVOLUTION

THE HEADQUARTERS OF THE MUNICIPALITY OF PARIS SINCE 1357

CITÉ INTERNATIONALE DES ARTS
18 RUE DE l'HÔTEL DE VILLE

COMMUNARDS SET FIRE TO THE
, LEAVING ONLY A STONE
HICH WAS
IN 1873-92

HÔTEL DE VILLE

66 Quai de l'Hôtel de ville

13-15
RUE FRANÇOIS
MIRON

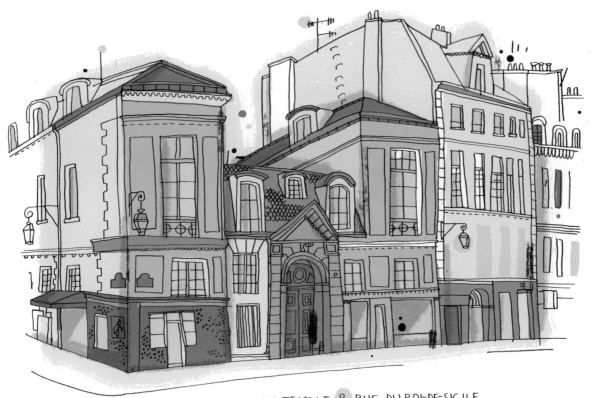

RUE VIELLE DU TEMPLE & RUE DU ROI-DE-SICILE

PLACE DES VOSGES

BUILT DURING HENRY IV'S REIGN FROM 1605-12 AS A MODEL FOR ROYAL CITY PLANNING

30 RUE
FRANÇOIS
MIRON

Izraël

MUSÉE
PICASSO
AT HÔTEL SAL

125
RUE
SAINT-
ANTOINE

2 RUE DES
HOSPITALIÈRES-
SAINT-GERVAIS

IN 1830 DURING THE REVOLUTION, A CANNONBALL GOT STUCK IN THE WALL & REMAINS THERE TODAY.

ERECTED BETWEEN 1474-1519 FOR THE ARCHBISHOP OF SENS

HÔTEL DE SENS
MARAIS.

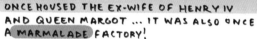

ONCE HOUSED THE EX-WIFE OF HENRY IV AND QUEEN MARGOT ... IT WAS ALSO ONCE A MARMALADE FACTORY!

OPÉRA BASTILLE

A MODERN OPERA HOUSE OPENED IN 1989 DESIGNED BY CARLOS OTT

ORIGINALLY THE SITE OF THE BASTILLE PRISON, WHICH WAS STORMED & THEN DESTROYED DURING THE FRENCH REVOLUTION.

THE PRISON HAD A BAD REPUTATION. AS A PLACE TO DUMP POLITICAL PRISONERS.

THE JULY COLUMN COMMEMORATES THE EVENTS OF THE JULY REVOLUTION.

PLACE DE LA BASTILLE

PONT MARIE

ORIGINALLY HOUSES WERE BUILT ON THE BRIDGE.

ITS NAME COMES FROM THE ENGINEER CHRISTOPHE MARIE.

BUILT BETWEEN 1614-35

ONE OF THE OLDEST BRIDGES IN PARIS

5TH ARR.

47-83 BOULEVARD DE L'HÔPITAL

GRAND MOSQUE OF PARIS

2 BIS PLACE DU PUITS DE L'ERMITE

FOUNDED IN 1926 AS GRATITUDE TO FRENCH MUSLIMS WHO FOUGHT AND DIED IN WORLD WAR ONE.

SHAKESPEARE AND COMPANY

37 RUE DE L'A BÛCHERIE

OPENED IN 1951

ORIGINALLY NAMED "LE MISTRAL"

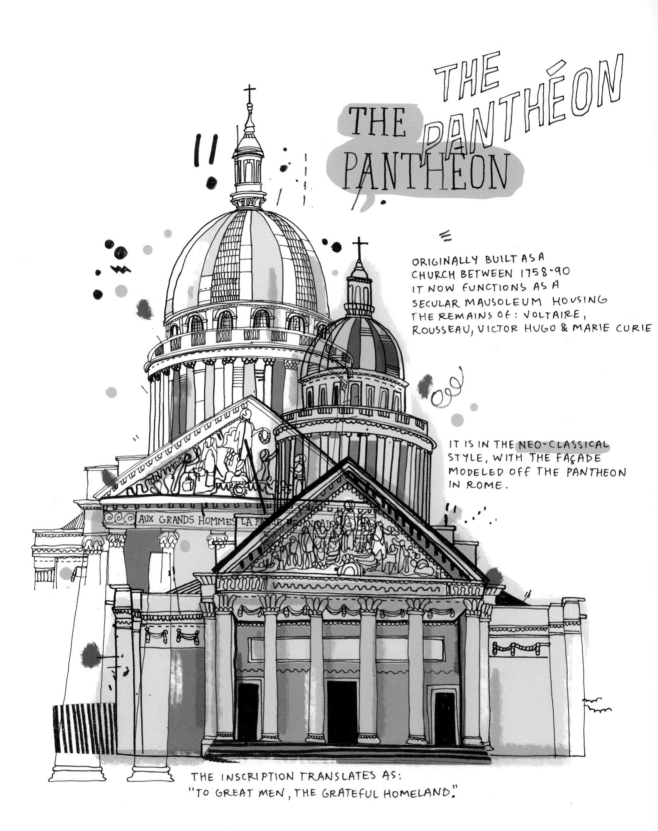

THE PANTHÉON

THE PANTHÉON

ORIGINALLY BUILT AS A CHURCH BETWEEN 1758-90 IT NOW FUNCTIONS AS A SECULAR MAUSOLEUM HOUSING THE REMAINS OF: VOLTAIRE, ROUSSEAU, VICTOR HUGO & MARIE CURIE

IT IS IN THE NEO-CLASSICAL STYLE, WITH THE FAÇADE MODELED OFF THE PANTHEON IN ROME.

AUX GRANDS HOMMES LA PATRIE RECONNAISSANTE

THE INSCRIPTION TRANSLATES AS:
"TO GREAT MEN, THE GRATEFUL HOMELAND."

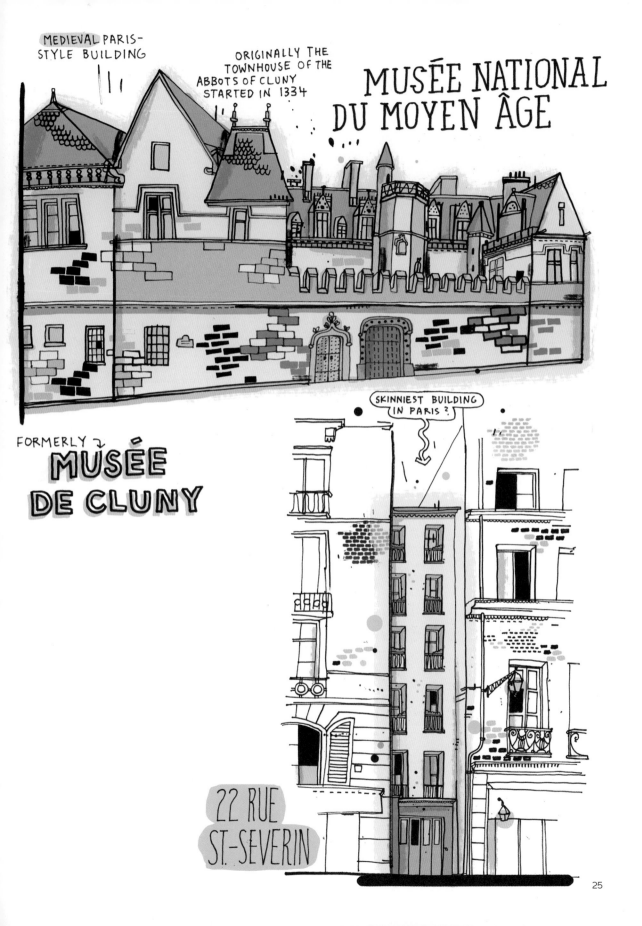

MEDIEVAL PARIS-STYLE BUILDING

ORIGINALLY THE TOWNHOUSE OF THE ABBOTS OF CLUNY STARTED IN 1334

MUSÉE NATIONAL DU MOYEN ÂGE

FORMERLY

MUSÉE DE CLUNY

SKINNIEST BUILDING IN PARIS?

22 RUE ST-SEVERIN

ABBAYE
DE SAINT-
GERMAIN-
DES-PRÉS

FOUNDED IN THE
6TH CENTURY

15 RUE DE VAUGIRARD

LUXEMBOURG PALACE

ORIGINALLY BUILT BETWEEN 1615–45

ARCHITECT SALOMON DE BROSSE DESIGNED IT AS THE ROYAL RESIDENCE. IT IS NOW THE SEAT OF THE FRENCH SENATE

MAISON DE VERRE CHAREAU

(HOUSE OF GLASS)

7TH ARR.

AN EXAMPLE OF EARLY MODERNISM EMPHASIZING AN HONESTY OF MATERIALS AND TRANSPARENCY OF FORMS.

BECAME A SALON FOR MARXIST INTELLECTUALS LIKE WALTER BENJAMIN

BUILT FROM 1928–32

31 RUE ST-GUILLAUME

RUE DU BAC

IT HOUSES THE LARGEST COLLECTION OF IMPRESSIONIST MASTERPIECES IN THE WORLD.

MUSÉE D'ORSAY

HOUSED IN A FORMER BEAUX-ARTS RAILWAY STATION FROM 1900.

PASSERELLE LÉOPOLD
SÉDAR-SENGHOR

BUILT IN 1997-99
UNDER MARC MIMRAM

129
RUE DE
GRENELLE

MUSÉE de
l'ARMÉE

THE NATIONAL
MILITARY MUSEUM OF
PARIS.

29 AVE. RAPP

BUILT IN
1901

A FRENCH ARCHITECT KNOWN FOR HIS ART NOUVEAU BUILDINGS

JULES LAVIROTTE
BUILDING

THE TOWER IS PAINTED EVERY 7 YEARS USING 60 TONS OF PAINT.

IT WAS THE TALLEST BUILDING IN THE WORLD FOR 41 YEARS UNTIL THE CHRYSLER BUILDING WAS BUILT.

324 METERS HIGH (1062 FEET)

NAMED AFTER GUSTAVE EIFFEL, WHOSE COMPANY DESIGNED & BUILT THE TOWER IN 1889.

EIFFEL TOWER

MADE FROM WROUGHT IRON

RODIN USED THE BUILDING AS HIS
WORKSHOP AND DONATED HIS
AND OTHER ARTIST'S WORKS TO
THE STATE.

THE THINKER
IS HERE AS
WELL AS WORKS
BY MONET,
RENOIR AND
VAN GOGH

MUSÉE RODIN

79 RUE DE VARENNE

OPENED IN 1919 DEDICATED
TO THE WORKS
OF AUGUSTE
RODIN.

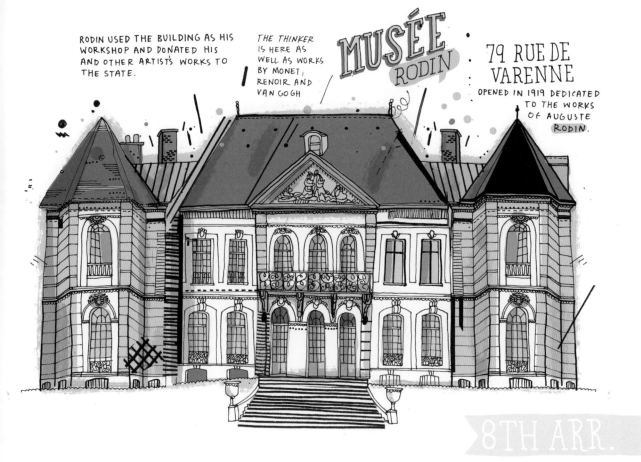

8TH ARR.

THÉÂTRE DES CHAMPS-ÉLYSÉES

DESIGNED BY
AUGUSTE
PERRET

BUILT FROM REINFORCED
CONCRETE IN THE
ART DECO STYLE...

.15 AVENUE MONTAIGNE

OPENED IN 1913

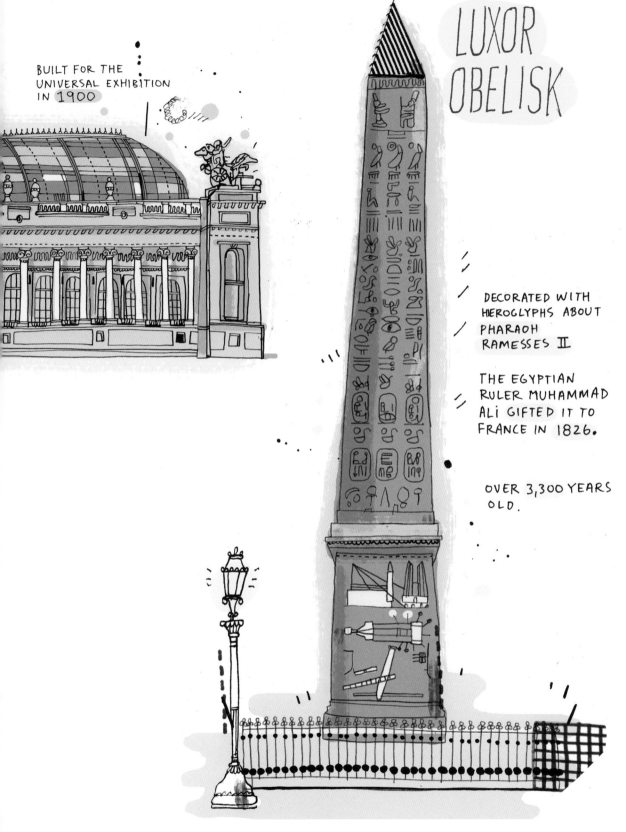

BUILT FOR THE UNIVERSAL EXHIBITION IN 1900

LUXOR OBELISK

DECORATED WITH HIEROGLYPHS ABOUT PHARAOH RAMESSES II

THE EGYPTIAN RULER MUHAMMAD ALI GIFTED IT TO FRANCE IN 1826.

OVER 3,300 YEARS OLD.

ARC DE TRIOMPHE

50 METERS TALL
(164 FEET)

BENEATH IS THE
TOMB OF THE
UNKNOWN
SOLDIER.

HONORS THOSE WHO FOUGHT AND DIED
FOR FRANCE IN THE FRENCH REVOLUTIONARY
AND NAPOLEONIC WARS.

PAGODE ROUGE

48 RUE DE COURCELLES

HEADQUARTERS OF THE LUXURY BRAND LOUIS VUITTON

101 AVENUE DES CHAMPS-ÉLYSÉES

34
AVENUE
DE WAGRAM

119 RUE
SAINT-LAZARE

CERAMIC HOTEL

McDonald's

McDonald's

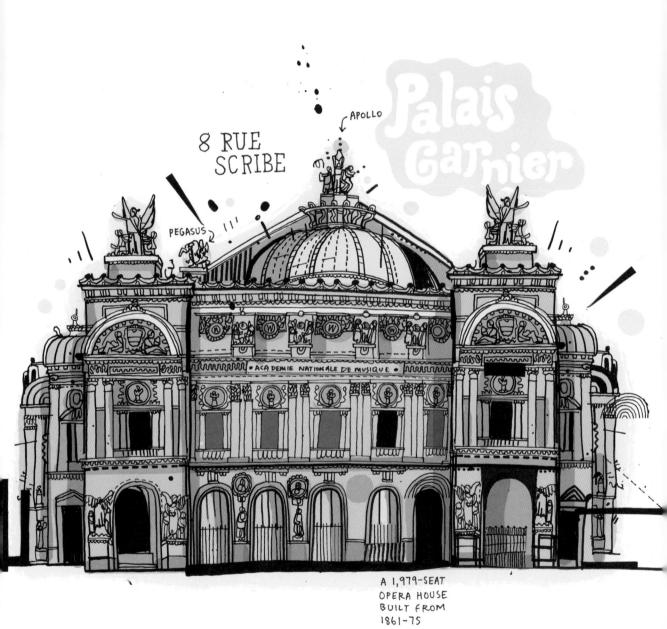

Palais Garnier

APOLLO

8 RUE SCRIBE

PEGASUS

ACADEMIE NATIONALE DE MUSIQUE

A 1,979-SEAT
OPERA HOUSE
BUILT FROM
1861-75

BOULEVARD HAUSSMANN

7 RUE DU FAUBOURG MONTMARTRE

32 RUE RICHER

A CABARET MUSIC HALL ESTABLISHED IN 1869

FOLIES BERGERE

DESIGNED BY JULES AND PAUL SEDILLE

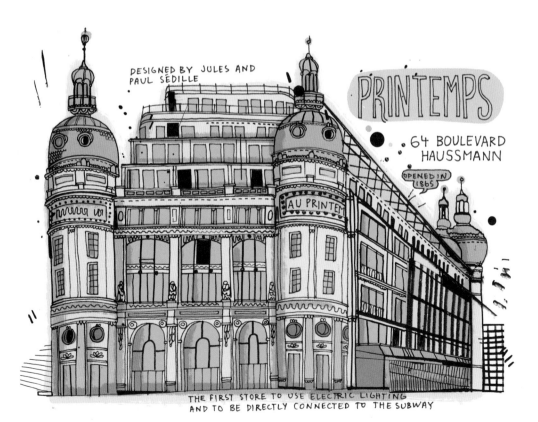

PRINTEMPS

64 BOULEVARD HAUSSMANN

OPENED IN 1865

AU PRINTE

THE FIRST STORE TO USE ELECTRIC LIGHTING AND TO BE DIRECTLY CONNECTED TO THE SUBWAY

NORD

1 BOULEVARD POISSONNIÈRE

REX

AN ART DECO LANDMARK

LARGEST CINEMA IN EUROPE

REX

REX

REX CLUB

18 RUE DE DUNKERQUE

GARE DU NORD

PASSAGE BRADY

33 BOULEVARD DE STRASBOURG

72 RUE DU FAUBOURG SAINT-MARTIN

7 RUE DU CHÂTEAU D'EAU

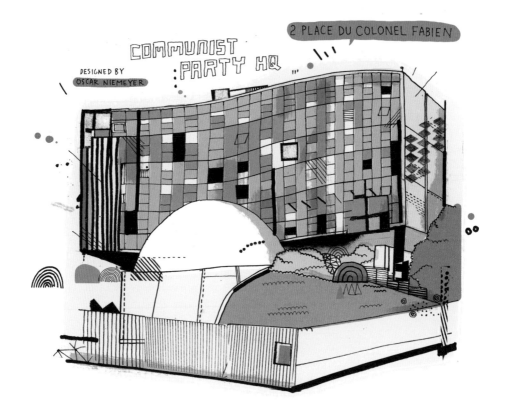

2 RUE MARIE ET LOUISE

110 RUE AMELOT

CIRQUE DHIVER

DESIGNED BY JACQUES
IGNACE HITTORFF &
OPENED BY EMPEROR
NAPOLEON III IN 1852

BUILT FOR
THE UNIVERSAL EXPOSITION
IN 1900

GARE
DE
LYON

HANDLES APPROX. 90 MILLION
PASSENGERS PER YEAR.

1 RUE
THEOPHILE
ROUSSEL

MARKET AT
SQUARE ARMAND
TROUSSEAU

13TH ARR.

80 AVENUE
DAUMESNIL

POLICE HQ FOR
THE 12TH ARRONDISSEMENT

DESIGNED IN 1991
THE FIGURES ON THE TOP
ARE REPLICAS OF MICHELANGELO'S
"THE DYING SLAVE."

LES DOCKS

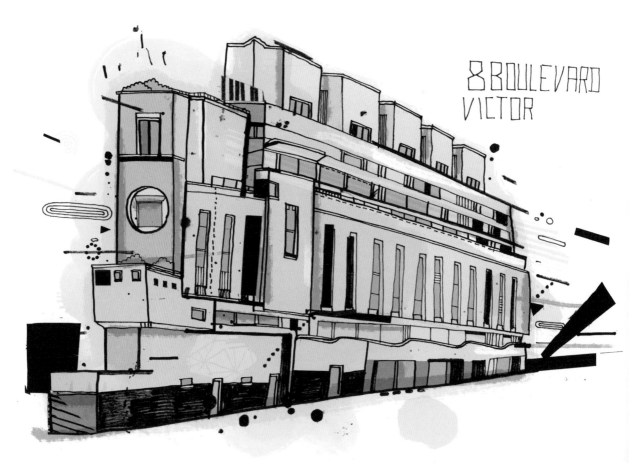

8 BOULEVARD VICTOR

MONTPARNASSE LIGHTHOUSE.

OWNER HUBERT BELLANGER BUILT THE LIGHTHOUSE TO PROMOTE THE FISH MARKET BELOW, "THE MIRACULOUS FISH".

HALLE AUX HUITRES

PLACE VICTOR-ET-HÉLÈNE-BASCH

LE ZEYER

DESIGNED IN THE
ART NOUVEAU
STYLE,
WHICH WAS INFLUENCED
BY NATURAL & ORANIC FORMS

24 PLACE ÉTIENNE-
PERNET

Restaurant

DESIGNED BY
AUGUSTE PERRET

25 bis RUE BENJAMIN
FRANKLIN

CHURCH
OF
SAINTE-ODILE

2 AVENUE
STÉPHANE MALLARMÉ

2 RUE de L'ABREUVOIR

82 BOULEVARD DE CLICHY

KNOWN AS THE BIRTHPLACE OF THE CAN-CAN, AND FOR INTRODUCING CABARET TO EUROPE

moulin de la Galette

ALSO KNOWN AS BLUTE FIN
IT WAS BUILT IN 1622

IMMORTALIZED IN RENOIR'S
PAINTING *BAL DU MOULIN DE
LA GALETTE*

BUILT FROM TRAVERTINE STONE
WHICH EXUDES CALCITE THAT KEEPS
THE BUILDING WHITE

BASILIQUE DU
SACRÉ-
COEUR

FUNDED MOSTLY
BY PUBLIC FUNDS WITH
PEOPLE PAYING FOR A BRICK
OR A COLUMN

SITUATED AT THE TOP
OF MONTMARTRE, THE
HIGHEST POINT OF THE
CITY.

CONSTRUCTION
BEGAN IN 1875 AN
WAS FINISHED IN
1914

PÈRE-LACHAISE CEMETERY

16 RUE DU REPOS

OSCAR WILDE IS BURIED HERE.

SPES · ILLORVM
IMMORTALITATE
PLENA · EST

QVI CREDIT IN ME
ETIAM SI MORT VVS
FVERIT VIVET

THE LARGEST CEMETERY IN PARIS

NOISY-LE-GRAND

LES ARÈNES DE PICASSO
AT NOISY-LE-GRAND

DESIGNED BY MANUEL NUÑEZ YANOWSKY

FONDATION Louis VUITTON

DESIGNED BY FRANK GEHRY, OPENED IN 2014

CITÉ DES SCIENCES
ET DE l'INDUSTRIE

30 AVENUE CORENTIN CARIOU

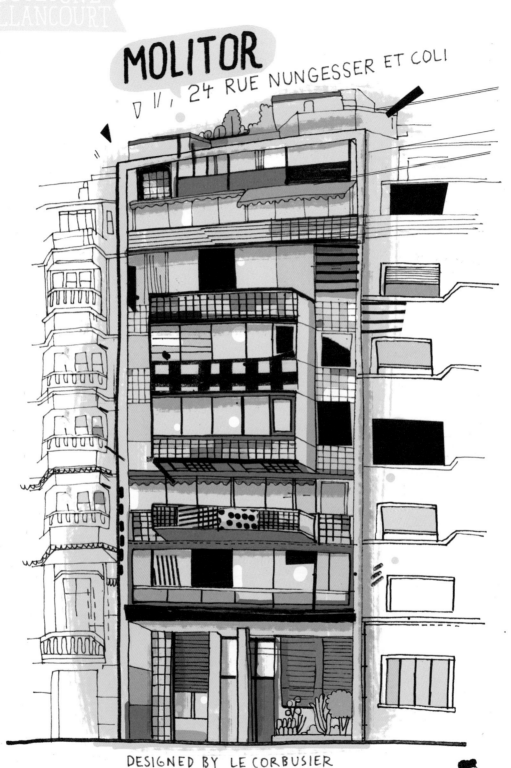

BOULOGNE-BILLANCOURT

MOLITOR

24 RUE NUNGESSER ET COLI

DESIGNED BY LE CORBUSIER

LA GRANDE ARCHE

DE LA DÉFENSE

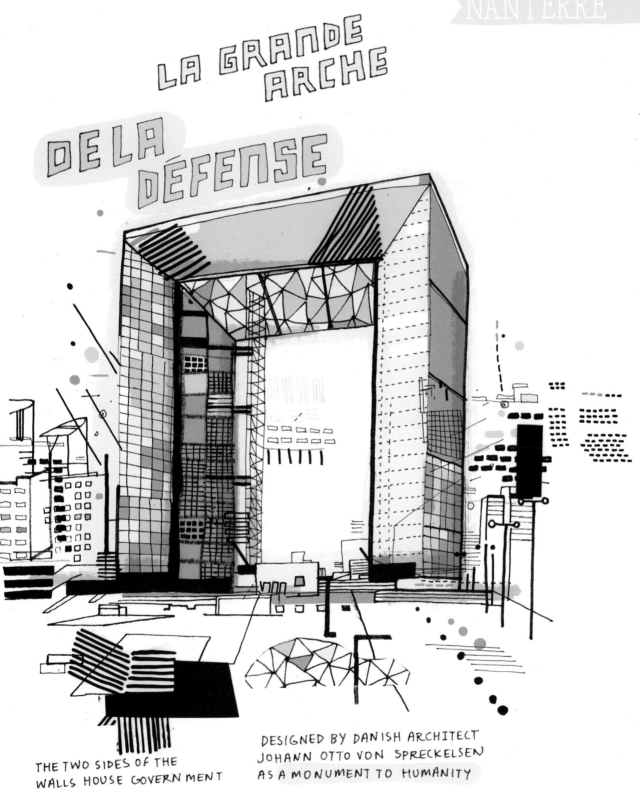

THE TWO SIDES OF THE
WALLS HOUSE GOVERNMENT
OFFICES.

DESIGNED BY DANISH ARCHITECT
JOHANN OTTO VON SPRECKELSEN
AS A MONUMENT TO HUMANITY

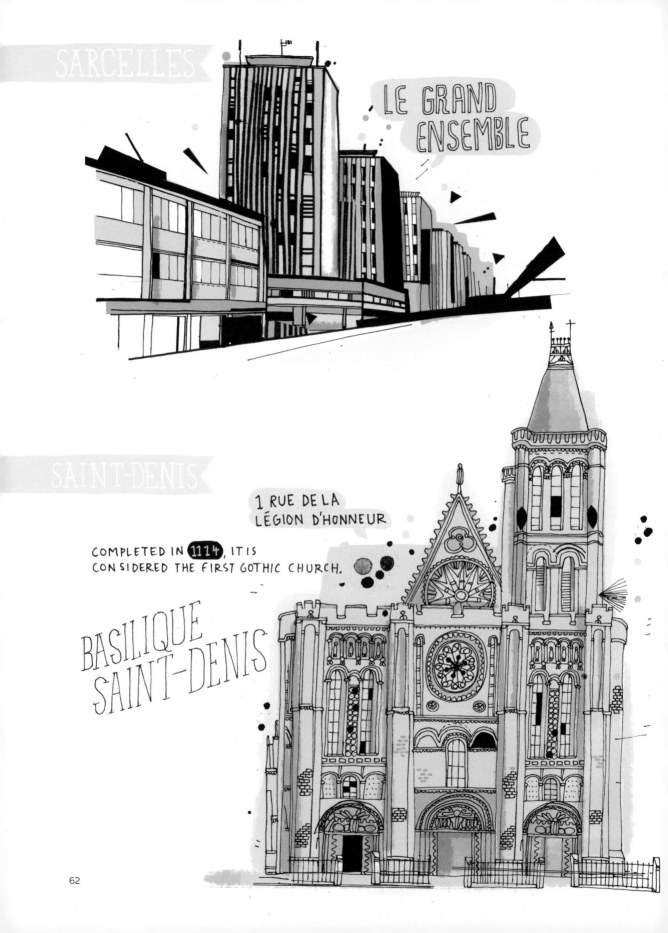

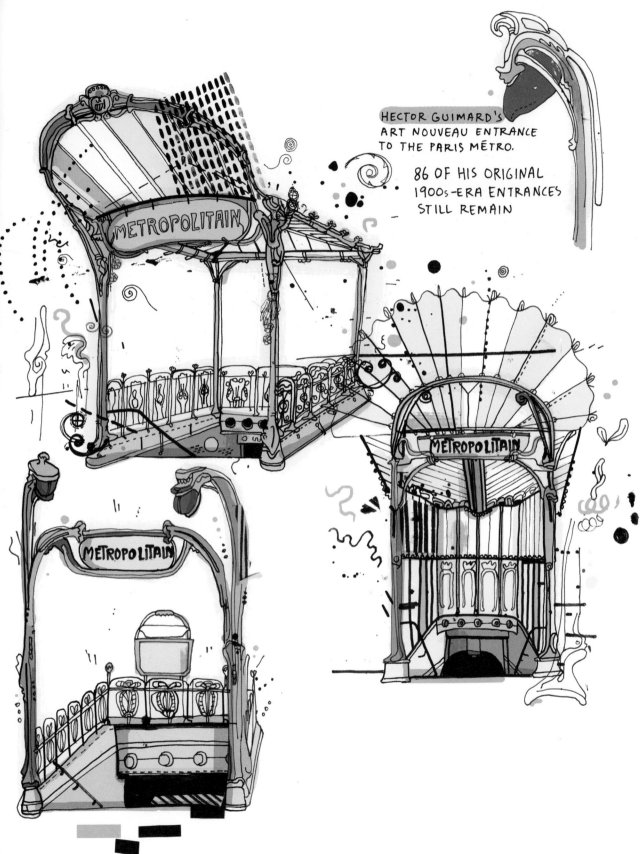

HECTOR GUIMARD'S
ART NOUVEAU ENTRANCE
TO THE PARIS MÉTRO.

86 OF HIS ORIGINAL
1900s-ERA ENTRANCES
STILL REMAIN

METROPOLITAIN

METROPOLITAIN

METROPOLITAIN

Thanks to Paris for being so delicious. Also thanks to all the people who gave me tips on places to draw: Anton Gill, Anna Brones, Lee Tran Lam, Aisha Ronniger, Jayne Tuttle, and Lisa Warner.

Designed and Illustrated by James Gulliver Hancock

First published in the United States of America in 2017 by
UNIVERSE PUBLISHING
A Division of Rizzoli International Publications, Inc.
300 Park Avenue South
New York, NY 10010
www.rizzoliusa.com

2017 2018 2019 2020 / 10 9 8 7 6 5 4 3 2 1

ISBN: 9780789334237

Library of Congress Control Number: 2017949054

Printed in China